BEDTIME STORIES FOR ADULTS

Relaxing Sleep Stories for Stressed-Out Adults, Powerful Guided Meditation to Defeat Insomnia, Reduce Anxiety and Sleep Smarter - Say Goodbye to Sleepless NIghts!

By

Elliott J. Power

TABLE OF CONTENTS

Thanks again for choosing this book, make sure to leave a short review on Audible if you enjoy it. I'd really love to hear your thoughts

INTRODUCTION

The stories you are about to read through will take you on journeys through different times and different realms. Sink deep into each tale as you see new forms of animals, dance the night away, take a stroll through space, listen to the woods, help a wizard find his pupil, and other stories. Curl up with this good book and read yourself to sleep.

CHAPTER 1

INTRO TO DREAMS:

There was a soft scratching at the door. The window bolted tight, the dog curled up on the bed, and the dog's owner, buried beneath layers of sheet and comforter. They ignored the initial scratching, rolling over away from the bedroom door, to face the wall and let slumber take them.

The pillows had just the right firmness to them, not too firm that it craned the neck, and not too flat that it felt as if nothing was there. The bed was perfectly supporting the body, and sleep could not be interrupted, not even by a strange noise. If they shifted the blankets too much, then they would get cold again, or maybe too warm if a foot became covered. The level of comfort achieved could not be disturbed.

There was another scratch at the door, followed by

a soft thump. This time, the dog sat up, staring at the door, it's body motionless. A low bark came from the dog as the scratching continued, more hurriedly now. Something wanted in. They ignored the dog; they ignored the scratching and closed their eyes tighter. However, the more they ignored it, the more persistent the sounds at the door became. Thumps followed by scrapes against the wood.

The dog let out a deeper bark, standing on all fours, at the foot of the bed, ears back and tail tucked between its legs. What creature could it be at this hour? Pushing the dog aside, they rise reluctantly from their bed, light activating automatically to fill the room from their movement. They approach the door, ready to face whatever nuisance lay beyond its frame.

A cat. The furry body intertwines with their legs, brushing against them with serene intensity. It was too late for such visits, but they acknowledge the cat, all the same, running their fingers through the soft long fur, evoking purrs and little mewls. They invite the cat to bed, the dog already laying back down, the feeling of danger having passed.

As the cat advances to the bed, the form changes, shifting from all fours, to stand tall, white fur turning to fair skin, and black spots becoming loose curls atop its head. Shorts are thrown at the grown man, standing before them. He was invited into sleep, no sense being as naked as a jaybird in the middle of the room. Crawling back into bed, the transformed man joins them, wrapping comforting arms around them. The purring remains despite the human shape, a nuzzle to the back of their neck as the cat-man settles in. The comfort from before had seemed perfect, but this new state curled up into his chest, would be even better. The sweetest of dreams were to come.

The room drifted away to be replaced by darkness and in that darkness, images came to them. Flashes of twisted memories, replayed in different settings, or with people they hadn't seen in years. Carried away through a vortex of stars to half-remembered worlds, and new ones entirely. Some dreams play out like a television show while in others you're the star even if you are not who you are supposed to be.

CHAPTER 2
THE BALL

Carriages arrived at the castle doors in procession, the people pouring from the decorative coaches, were prepared for a masquerade. Everyone wore a different color, and a mask to match their elaborate outfits. Full skirts, formal suits, sleek gowns, fluttered through the doors, giggling with the events to come. The masks themselves represented different animals, various ones of fine and elaborate design.

A masked fox fluttered in an orange ball-gown, the fluff of the dress contrary to the speed and slyness a fox usually showed. Her long black tresses were loose and springs of curl dutifully in place from the wand of a hot iron. She danced along to the tune, twirling about by herself, and filled the room.

A band on the stage wore simple black and white uniforms, their masks that of similar creatures:

penguins, zebras, white tigers, ferrets, skunks, and a cow playing the stand-up bass. The melody carried through the grand room and carried out into the garden, visible through the large double doors to a small balcony.

The enchanting fox twirled and twirled until she felt the cool night air again, dancing her way from the ball-room floor to the low balcony. She had danced past masks of fowls, deer, reptiles, any number of creatures one might find in the forest or hills. It was only when she braced herself against the banister that she stopped dancing, catching her breath and laughing softly. She tilted her head back, soaking in the bright moonlight and relishing in the feel of freedom.

“You dance beautifully,” mused a wolf to her left, his suit was silver and black, to match the mask he wore, his features foxlike but larger and darker.

“Thank you, stranger,” the fox returned, offering him a curtsy.

"Would you honor me with a dance?" He stepped closer to her; his arm stretched out to her. She blushed beneath her mask, sizing up the wolf, much taller than her but lean and agile like her kind. She nodded and lightly placed a gloved hand on his forearm as he led her back inside.

The instruments started slowly, allowing the couples time to bring themselves onto the floor. A peacock was paired with an owl, a snake with a hare, and to their left a fawn with a moose antler, outrageous with their masks. They circled slowly, eyes deeply penetrating one another as they held each other in the musical embrace. Gradually, the music picked up the pace until each couple was a whirl of mixed hues, and cheers from the observing crowd encouraged their efforts.

The fox with her bright hazel eyes stared into the cold blue eyes across from her, even as they whirled about with speed and complexity – she never took her eyes off him. He handled her with firm grace, leading her into each move with expertise while she progressed into the next move without thought. Soon the floor was empty except for the fox and wolf, the other couples yielding to their chemistry and finesse.

The music ended on a crescendo, there was a brief pause of silence, the fox and the wolf breathing heavily, and then roaring cheers followed. The two bashfully bowed and nodded their heads before escaping to the outdoors once more. The wolf snatched two glasses from a passing gazelle, a silver platter with a variety of beverages. He sniffed the two and smiled.

"Champagne or Sangria?" he inquired, holding out the two tall flutes.

"Sangria," The fox took the ruby-colored flute and took a sip, sighing at the sweetness. "I like the fruit," she replied.

"I thought foxes ate meat." He took a long drink, nearly finishing his glass and smiled down at her.

"Doesn't mean I can't enjoy the sweeter things in life. I like the hen house as much as the blackberry bush." She took her time, tasting the drink, relishing her soft lips against the cool glass.

"Do you ever wish it was more than one night a year?" The wolf turned away from the ballroom to peer over the enchanted garden.

"The ball or the form?" She finished held her glass delicately and leaned over the railing.

"The chance to do it more than once…when we want to would be better than a single night." He finished his sparkling wine and licked his lips. He reached out slowly and brushed his bare knuckles across her gloved hand.

"Perhaps." She glanced at their touching hands and her face softened beneath the mask. "What has you wishing to be human, my dear wolf?"

"A chance to see you more than one evening." There was a deep longing in his voice.

"You do. I see you in the wood, amongst your pack…" She left off other details, of who she saw him with. "Walk with me." She set her unfinished drink down and took his hand into hers, leading him towards the small staircase.

He let her guide him away from the cheerful music to the peace and beauty of the garden. Pillars of garden greenery were carved in shapes of woodland creatures, and paths were lined with rose bushes, a trickling pond filling the length of the center. They walked a short while, hand in hand, the fox and the wolf. He stopped them both suddenly, drawing her close to him, arm about her waist and the other still clasped in hers. They locked eyes, her gaze searching his for answers while his delved into her soul. He kissed her, intensely but not with force, his intentions thick with yearning. The fox pulled back after her moments of desire and shook her head, tears slipping from her eyes.

"We cannot," she whispered. "But I will cherish

these nights." He was quiet as he held her close, basking in the feel of her form against his. Resigned, the fox rested her damp cheek to his shoulder and breathed in his scent.

They remained together for the evening until the moon slid away beyond the trees, the party guests long gone, whisked away in their carriages to be turned into fractured coaches, broken along old and forgotten roads. As the sun rose, the full moon gone, a little red fox, and a gray wolf parted ways amidst the overgrown grounds.

There would be next year and the two could share a dance again. The fox returning to her hovel and hen house to bother. The wolf returned to his pack, to his mate and litter.

CHAPTER THREE

CITIZEN OF ADIS

Deep breath in. Deep breath out. Don't panic, just breath. The floating sensation will feel like your new normal soon. The gravity here is lighter, the air a purer form of oxygen until you get into the city blocks," the voice above reassures you as you pull your body from the capsule. "Welcome to Outpost Adis."

Your body feels lighter as you step onto the cold metal surface, your shoes not necessary during the cryosleep. The last time you had walked anywhere, was a little blue and green planet, light-years away. Feeling a little high on the oxygen you stumble your way through the room to the far wall, to the sign indicating a place to shower and change. The voice continued without prompting, a recording of welcome to its newest citizen.

"You have traveled across time and space for your

new life here on Outpost Adis. The satellite housing rotates around the plant Adis below. Adis is a lush green world, with 90% of its surface lying beneath mineral-rich waters. Trips to Adis's surface are limited for leave and supply expeditions." There was a brief pause. "You have two-hundred and thirteen days of leave available." It was reading your profile to assess the information. "This has been converted to two-hundred and thirteen hours of leave available on Adis' surface. As a citizen here, you have access to libraries, mess halls, and all classrooms. Your quarters are located in sector 23, block B. Additional access will have to be requested from your block leader."

After a refreshing shower and a fresh change of clothes, you test out your space-legs and stroll through sectors you have permission to enter. While the halls are made of dense metal, the surroundings do not feel claustrophobic nor cold – a hominess about it, as people pass and nod in greeting to you. There are different uniforms according to people's jobs. You sport simple yellow breeches and billowy shirt, the color of a new citizen, this will notify others of your inexperience in space as well as be ready to answer any questions you may have. There are blue tighter uniforms for those that worked directly on the space station such as engineers and pilots. The red uniforms are for experienced citizens who had lived there for more than a year, a rite of passage for some. As a new citizen, the yellow is comforting for you, a symbol of your new beginning.

You stop to stare out of a hull, the view is breathtaking. The scenery is pitch black but speckled with stars, no light pollution in sight. There you can see the arms of galaxies, the oblong shapes of the moons around Adis, and the planet below as well. Hues of teal blue, with tinges of pink, and patches of dark forest green, it is easy to spot the flora and the beaches from the extensive water surface.

Your new life settles in with ease, getting used to your surroundings and committing the hallways to memory to not get lost. They ask for any volunteers for a spacewalk and you leap at the chance. They pick a small handful and take you to an airlock. There you change from your yellow clothes to a suit of vivid white. Others around you change out of red and yellow clothes, only the two in charge of the spacewalk are in blue. The white uniforms are explained to stand out in contrast to dark space, in case you are separated for whatever reason. You are briefly taught how to control your breathing, how to read your suit levels.

The spacesuit is heavier than your clothes and the weight is reassuring because of the lack of gravity beyond the airlock doors. You grin and stand in line as the blues, lock everyone into a secured line, a pipe-like rope that hooks to your waist – further safety precautions. There is a signal, a red light turns green, and the doors open. There is a tug against your body as air is emptied from the room.

Your heart hammers briefly in your chest as you come to meet with eternity, but it slows as you practice your breathing exercises and the line moves. The weight of the suit is barely noticeable, as the group floats out. You are guided with the others without walking, strung along by your safety line.

You're signaled to activate the magnets in your boots as you're guided to the surface of the housing satellite. You sink until a dull thud resonates through your feet as metal meets boots. You're able to walk freely now, slack provided in the safety rope. Eagerly, you stroll away from the small gathering to stand on the edge of a panel, overlooking the great abyss.

Insignificance briefly enters your mind as you stare into the star-filled depths. It quickly melts away as you admire your situation, a chance at a new life, a new world. Insignificance turns into meaning, you have been given the chance to start again among stars, new worlds. You relax your body and lift your arms, and the magnets keep you planted as your body rocks to the waves and breeze of the cosmos.

CHAPTER FOUR
FLIGHT OF THE OWL

The window opens slowly, a beak and claws pawing at the clasp. A soft hoot fills the room. I'm already waiting for the creature. I scrambled to him, my bed abandoned hours ago. There was always too much excitement buzzing inside of me to even try to get a wink of sleep. The owl came at midnight every two weeks to take me away.

It was a large beast of the air, it's body the shape of a barrel of feathers featuring beige and fleshy pinks, streaked with burgundy, and black strips along the wings. He stood on the roof, much too large to fit through the window he came to during his visits. Wide yellow eyes peered at me unblinking, impatient with me even as I was taking off my bathrobe to accompany him outside. I bowed low to him when I balanced standing on the rickety shingles.

"Where to tonight?" I ask, knowing an unintelligible hoot would be the response.

He shuffled to the edge, a nervous twitch of his wings beckoning me closer. This part was always the hardest. I swallowed and made my way behind him and pressed into the feathers. His head twisted to face me, an affectionate peck to the top of my head. I buried my fingers into the feathers and felt the reigns, somehow always there when I searched for them. I gripped tightly and exhaled slowly, pressing against him.

His neck snapped forward and he took a swooping dive off the high roof. I swallowed my scream of momentary fright before looking up, the gush of air making my eyes water. He was as tall as me but even wider as his wingspan was twice my size. He flapped and soared, keeping a level to his flight as we approached the edge of the wood. I inhale sharply, thinking his wingspan too large for the gaps between the trees. I clutch tightly to my reigns and my knees dig into his sides as he turns, the inverted angle allows him to make room. He flies down, and we pass through an even narrower tree line.

My eyes water and small branches lick my skin, but I hardly notice, the euphoria of flight enthralling me in its grips. I can only hear the whoosh of the wind and the warmth of the body of the Owl pressed into mine. It feels like we are one, though I have no control, a passenger on the back of this feathered beast. He speeds deeper and deeper until he finds a perch on a branch sturdy enough for the weight of the two of us.

I'm breathless as I slide off his back to lean against the trunk, feet settled on the curve of the branch. Once the pounding of my heart in my ears has settled, I could hear the woods alive around me. Wolves howled at the moon I could not see, the thick canopy blocking my view. My traveling companion hooted and gestured his wing downward. I took a seat on the branch, thanking them. Settled in more, I closed my eyes and could hear frogs croaking in a pond somewhere close. Crickets played a tune on the fiddles that were their legs. The scurried sounds of squirrels, not yet asleep, as they shimmied up trees. Raccoons chirped at one another as they foraged for berries.

It was a great contrast to the city sounds I was so used it, the shouting of people late into the night, honking of horns, a train rushing by a few blocks away. My eyelids didn't lift, too heavy, as I was lullabied by the forest.

I was vaguely aware as the Owl lifted me and took me back through the skies. Nestled against his chest, listening to his soothing heartbeat, snug against his chest, as he made his way back to my home. I did not question how the swooping owl put me to bed each time, it perplexed me, sure, but so did flying with an owl once a fortnight. I did not want to question the good things, less I were to lose them. My bed was a weak replacement in comparison to the wings of my flying companion, but the song of the wood still rung in my ears, drowning out the humdrum of reality.

Muttering my thanks, the owl brushed my hair with its beak and left me to my sleep. Until next time, I would soar with him once more.

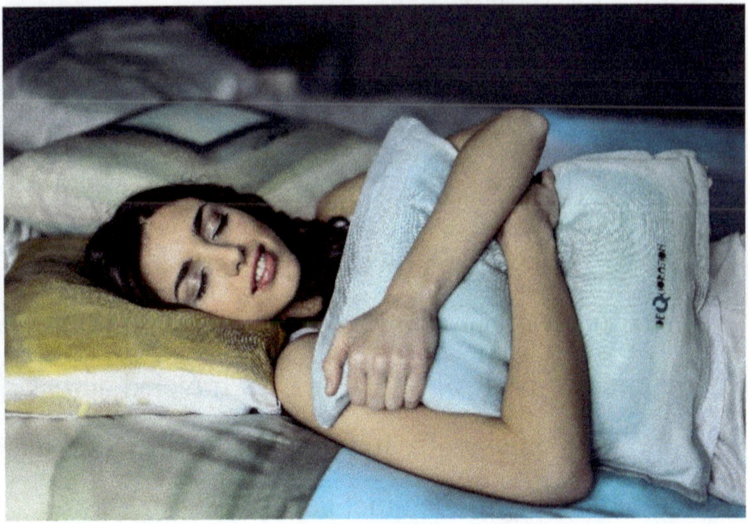

CHAPTER FIVE
THE LIBRARY

The stacks seemed endless. Their height only stopped by the ceiling, where on the next story more books sat waiting on shelves. Entering the vast library, the overwhelming scent of musty pages, dusty tomes, and fresh ink fill the senses.

A woman sits behind a large desk beyond the entrance, her glasses settled on the bridge of her nose. One might assume she was the librarian, but there were no stamps to allow books to leave their stacks. Instead, she had books piled up around her, one open in front of her. Her eyes traveled across every line quickly to turn the page, the simple motion echoing in the quiet halls.

She looked up, as if disturbed, to find you are standing before her. She tuts in disapproval, grabs a bookmark, and carefully marks her place in her book. She muttered about never bending a page or breaking the spine of the book, and closes it shut – the snap too, reverberates through the space. The woman mentions your late and steps out from behind her desk. She is a small stout woman, hair silvered with age, she moves with surprising agility for her age though, approaching you.

Sizing you up, she clicks her tongue, and it's hard to tell if it's in approval or disapproval. She motions you to follow her and your eyes are filled with the spines of books, the edges of scrolls, display podiums of open pages with illustrations that could bring one to tears. There is no dust for so many books having gone untouched, the air crisp with the scent of the parchment and ink. There is a soft hum hanging in the atmosphere that only grows as you are drawn deeper into the library.

The hum sounds like a collective of voices, not shouting over one another to be heard, but speaking the words of their pages. The stories murmuring their tales, facts, and anecdotes to anyone that might listen. You wish to stop but the woman leads you up a stairwell to the other floors, your footsteps joining in the undertones.

She finally stops at a desk, like hers but several stories up, and yet there is more library to explore above and below. She gestures to the chair behind the desk, offering it to you. You take it and sink into the worn cushions, it feels warm as if someone has only just left it. Neatly broken in, the chair is perfect, not a spring out of place, and the back support exquisite. There are already towers of books and bunches of scrolls across the surface. The older woman leaves you and disappears along the path that brought you here.

You grab a scroll, the texture like rough velvet under your fingers as you untie the binding. Languages you never knew you could read are crystal clear to you. You spend hours reading through the painted words, histories of people, and their dynasties. You finish your scrolls, your eyes not hurting, and your mind alight with information. You grab the closest book and begin to turn its pages. This one brings you to tears with its heart-wrenching storyline. You're not sure if you are reading faster than before or if time has no meaning here, you finish the book in what feels like no time and move on to the next.

The books never end, the stories never cease, and the words flow in such harmony. Heaven, a sanctuary of peace.

CHAPTER SIX
HOLIDAY TRADITIONS

Rocking around the Christmas tree…" played on the radio. It was the day after Thanksgiving, and tradition meant, it was Christmas time until New Year's Eve. As soon as the clock struck midnight radio stations blasted the countless songs of Christmas from old to new and would not stop till the cheer was run out of town.

Lights would be decorating houses soon and trees put up in living rooms. Trees of tinsel, trees of plastic, and trees of living wood, cut down from the farms. The Harrow's family would be cutting down their tree as they did every year, the day after Thanksgiving. Their living room had a dedicated spot against the stairwell, this spot allowed for maximum height, that pleased Mrs. Harrow most.

The whole family donned warm clothes from head

to toe. Large jackets, sturdy mittens, and scarves long enough to keep the ears warm. Mr. Harrow, however, always wore his trapper hat, the fur completely covering his ears, there was never enough warmth for those little appendages. The two children of the Harrows were an older girl and a younger boy: Lexi and Ryker. The two were eager for the tradition – a day of trekking through snow, cutting down a tree, peppermint sticks, and best of all, hot chocolate.

The Harrow family piled into their truck, Mrs. Harrow playing the songs of the season, and Mr. Harrow manning the wheel. Lexi leaned against the window, already setting out to sleep the whole car ride while Ryker sang unceremoniously along with the songs; barely knowing all the words.

They pulled up to the Tree Farm, lots of other families pulling in at the same time. The kids charged out of the truck, Mrs. Harrow hollering after them.

"They'll be fine," Mr. Harrow reassured their children beyond the age of needing direct supervision. The parents shared a brief kiss, a romantic whisper that normally would have provoked a 'blegh' from Ryker and got out of the vehicle themselves.

The hillsides were dusted with snow, the air thick with excitement for the holiday to come. The kids had run off to the hut with a bold sign labeled for beverages: namely hot chocolate and coffee. It was still early but that did not stop Lexi from sliding over a five-dollar bill and getting the two styrofoam cups of sweet memories. Lexi made her little brother beg for his cup before handing it over; he took a sip before letting it cool, yowled in pain. Without thinking, he grabbed a handful of snow and buried his burnt tongue in it. Lexi laughed and blew on her hot chocolate so as not to make the same mistake as Ryker.

Mr. Harrow found them after he picked out a saw.

and a wagon ride around a small Christmas village, while the folks paid for their Christmas tree. They laid the tree across the bed of the truck, leaving the tailgate open as the end stuck out – Mr. Harrow tied a yellow warning ribbon to it, for safety. Bungees in hand, they secured their bounty and made their way home.

Erected against the staircase in the foyer, the tree was a sight to behold. Mr. Harrow swore at tangled lights as he helped Mrs. Harrow wrap them around their tree. The tree-topper brushed the ceiling, a glowing star. During the first few weeks of December, the tree would be decorated with an assortment of ornaments, tied to a memory or colorful bargain bulbs secured from the Christmas sales.

On Christmas morning the tree would be even more bountiful, it's lights flashing in a programmed rhythm, as presents lay across the base. Stockings hung by the chimney, packed with little goodies,

Mrs. Harrow had been up all-night filling. The air filled with the scent of cinnamon rolls and coffee, as the Harrows rose to enjoy each other and the gifts they had picked out for one another with care.

CHAPTER SEVEN
THE WIZARD

High up in his tower, Galgamare looked over the lands where he practiced magic. The wizard was getting on in age and would need an apprentice soon. He withdrew from the window to his study, looking over his tomes, his enchanting circle, and apothecary he held dear to his heart. Determined to carry on his magical legacy, he sought out a pupil. He promised himself that the next day he would leave his tower to find himself a student.

He set out at daybreak after his breakfast. He carried a pack with him, a staff, and wore purple robes of good bulk – his traveling robes. It was two days' walk to the north before he came to his first town, a small village with a small market square and an inn that was really someone's home with an extra bedroom. He produced a booth from his magic pack, a small table, and a stool for him to sit on. Galgamare cleared his throat and waited to be approached; he had situated himself to sit in the middle of the village.

Various folk approached him through the day, inquiring his business there. Once they learned of the magic, a couple grew fearful, children giggled, and a few tried to hire him for odds and ends. He earned his free night at the "inn" with a few spells to return passed-their-time meats to their prime. It was simple and well-practiced magic to him; it was how he kept to himself so long in his tower. He kept food and water with ease while remaining alone.

While he broke bread with his hosts, he tried to think of the last time he was around so many people or anyone. They made small talk, the innkeeper and his wife, childless but hospitable people. When there were no travelers on the road to stay, they made their money-making brew for the town, various mead, and ales, no grapes or fruit for decent wine. They shared a potent ale with the wizard before he turned in for the evening.

No prospects in the small village with no name, Galgamare wished his hosts well and set out to the northwest for the next town. He had studied the maps to memory to find his way about the countryside. He did not want a city child; they saw wonders big and small far more than the country bumpkin did. He had been a child from a farm a very long time ago. As he walked, his mind slipped in and out of reality, recalling his first experiences with magic and how he began his path towards sorcery

He had been sixteen, working the fields, with dry soil to try and grow any bit of grain he could. A windmill that doubled as his home turned slowly, one of the flaps broken. He woke every morning before dawn to tend to the fields, herd the goats, and milk them. He fetched wild eggs from the surrounding nests and tended to any hens they owned. By daybreak, he was taking the milk and eggs to his mother and father in a small hut at the head of the farm.

His mother would greet him with a ruffle of his hair and retrieve the eggs from his arms. He set the bucket of milk down for his sister, who would make cheese with it when she rose from her bed. His father was still out hunting, he often went on small trips beyond the farm for better game. Breakfast cooking, Galgamare inquired where his sister was when she did not come at the smell of thick sizzling bacon and eggs. His mother urged him to pull the sleeping girl from bed, there was no time for laziness.

"She's gone," he told his mother, confused. "Her bed is empty like she never slept in it." He and his mother searched the farm for her, shouting for her but there was no sign. He ate the overcooked eggs and the burnt bacon in silence, his mother refusing to eat while she fretted. It hurt me to see my mother, a kind but stern woman, in such a fright. "I'll find her," he promised. "Stay here in case she comes home." My mother reluctantly agreed and gave the young man a small pouch of bread and cheese if he were to be gone for a long time.

Galgamere rechecked the farmstead and any known pockets in hillsides, trenches for water, but there was no sign of her on their land. He braved the wood next, calling out to her but never hearing back, he would shout as long as he could but would need to be quiet come nightfall. Desperate, Galgamere stopped by a stream and stared hard into the water, willing it to show where his sister was, just as it showed him his reflection. He remembered the fright and elation as he saw the reflection shift from his features to that of his sister's, a pretty girl with long hay colored hair; she looked well, arms around her as she leaned against the Jayson's boy, from the next farm. Mother would be infuriated.

He told her mother what he saw, and she looked pale, unsure whether to believe him or curse him. Sure enough, they found his sister on the neighboring farm in their small barn, kissing amongst the mares. When his father returned home, she'd had a stern talking to, and a betrothal to the boy she had been caught with. Galgamare on the other hand was packed with more rations and told to leave – there was no place for magicked children here.

He had wandered until his shoes wore and his feet bled, and he found the tower he called home. A woman had lived there at the time, young and vibrant with life and she had taught him all he knew until her dying breath. From there he took to studying alone, amongst his scrolls and artifacts, buying from passing adventurers who had loot that would serve his magic.

Galgamare squinted and spotted farms in the distance, lands neatly categorized by what they grew. He counted four within his vision and took to visiting each, offering his services and requesting to know of any children that may be gifted. While the first two had nothing for him, save for the curing of a lame calf, he was luckier at the third.

A small girl, younger than he had been when he'd discovered sorcery, with big violet eyes, was troubled with visions. The parents seemed fearful of the girl with raven hair and pale skin, a bruise across her chin, and knees.

"They're violent outbursts," explained the mother when Galgamare had shot her an accusing look. "When the visions strike her, she collapses where she is and has a seizure. Not right," she added.

He sighed and nodded, taking the girl's hands in his, observing the rough scratches from stopping herself falling. Inquiring what she saw, she explained in a tiny voice, she saw things that happened and didn't happen, futures, and possible futures. She even told him the secret of making a snake that had bit her dog disappear without so much as a thought.

"I would like to take her," Galgamare explained to her parents. They had seven children in total, all with blue eyes except for the little girl. Their mother had blue eyes, but the father had two mismatched eyes, a quiet man with one eye brown and the other purple. The woman of the household did most of the talking, negotiating when and why her daughter would be leaving them.

He gave them time to say their good-byes, the little girl was given fresh boots and a small satchel to carry her things. She stood as tall as Galgamare's hip but he knew she would grow just as her knowledge would of arcane magic. She sniffled and cried softly for a while, as they walked, neither speaking to the other.

"I think I will make this trip to your new home quicker, what say you?" She blinked, rubbing the tears from her eyes. "Help me make a portal?" Her eyes grew as big as saucers and agreed eagerly, extending her hands to him. He laughed at her spirit. He took her hand into his and held out his other, drawing circles and symbols in the air. “Copy me if you can,” he encouraged.

Her little brow furrowed, and her hand clumsily tried to draw in the air. While her ability to map out ruins was poor, he could feel the power resonating in her from the concentration and will. He had found a fine pupil on the farm. A burst of power popped in the air in front of him, a tear in reality as a new path was forged for them. It was a tall oval mirror that showed them a tall tower and a cobblestone path going from worn to untouched the closer to the tower it became.

“Home,” Galgamare told the girl who needed no prompting to skip through the portal, the green of the magic tinged with purple from the power borrowed from the farm-girl. Laughing he added, “A fine pupil indeed.”

There in his tower, he taught the girl everything she

knew. Her name was Morra, and she took to magic easily. He wished he had been so young when he was first taught, her mind pliable to lessons. Languages he had never heard spoken she took to like a fish to water. She did her first summon at nine years old and it was only the beginning.

CHAPTER EIGHT
ACROSS THE SEA

The ship pitched to and fro, the waves tossing it about with little mind to the small wooden thing in its depths. Men shouted at one another, orders flying by and being repeated, and then followed by confirmations of tasks complete. A captain stood at the wheel, turning it hard to drive his ship where he wanted. The sudden change in the rough waves were a sign they were close, they were coming to waters untouched, harmful, and protected by witchcraft. There was a small crew of those brave enough to join him. Among them you are brave enough to be aboard, not for the spirit of sailing the sea but because those protected waters held the dreams you were desperate to make a reality.

The waters turned from the dark blue to a vivid green, emerald hues twisting with turquoise. These were the colors you had seen in your dreams, the promise of life beneath them. The crew shouted after you as you stripped off your boots and dove into the water. The surface is warm and bubbly but as you sink further the cold grips you and your lungs burn. You try to swim for the surface, but you no longer know which way is up – you can no longer see the hull of the ship that had been above you moments ago.

Hands wrap around your ankles and tug, pulling you deeper and deeper. Your chest aches, your neck burns, the saltwater filling your lungs. You kick at the hands but still, you sink further and further, deeper and deeper.

You blink, the darkness becoming clear as your eyes adjust, the world tinted by a film of aquamarine. You inhale deeply, feeling a rush through your neck – touching it, you feel the slits of gills and the small air bubbles that leave them when you exhale. You cry triumphantly and kick in the water to swim – your legs are no longer two but one solid fin with scales from, red to orange to the yellow tip of the fin. You rip away the tatters of your trousers and tug off your shirt, free from the surface and embraced by the sea. You do flips and circle, take deep breaths, bewildered each time as you suck in water instead of air.

Remembering something or someone had pulled you down, you go searching, diving deeper to find the source of your welcoming. You dodge a school of fish, swimming past you as you dive, fight off free-flowing seaweed until you drift through open cracks and cliffs to settle on the sandy floor. From the floor, you pick a direction and set forth.

An old shipwreck is covered in barnacles off to your right. You move over to it and inspect the craft, split in two, with dark marks to indicate destruction by storms. You find a small cabin onboard, no treasure but an old bottle of wine. You pop the cork and watch the dark burgundy liquid fill the water around you. You inhale and it tickles and burns a little to breathe in the alcohol. You cough and shake, learning that breathing the ancient liquid was not the best of consumption methods.

Needing an answer, you leave the shipwreck to seek out your kind. There are more broken and cast aside debris of ships – a graveyard for those misunderstanding the sea and its warnings. You have embraced the waters and have been rewarded for your dreams.

You spot eyes across the way in a field of seaweed, tall, and shifting with the tides above, the silky grass looks pleasant. You swim over as fast as you can, still adjusting to your new body. You see tails of blue, green, and purple, other shades on each tail, their hair colors matching, some even have scales and fins decorating their arms. You shout in wonder and move to them, your questions countless and their humor good to you. They lead you further from the surface world, the cold of the water no longer a bother to you, the saltwater in your lungs your lifeblood, and your tail better than sea legs.

They take you into their city, their homes, whales decorate the ocean above like heavy set birds. Tall spiral structures stick out from the ground as large coral, carved out to house the merfolk. Shells decorated the people and houses alike, polished to shine like jewels. Pearls dangled from ears, recovered treasures from simple keepsakes such as silverware to decorate their homes.

You find yourself starting to gather your own.

CHAPTER NINE

THE DRAGON AND THE BOUNTY

High up in the hills, there lay a pitch-black dragon. She was a beast to behold that hunted the lands, eating creatures at pasture and unknowing humans alike. She was such a terror to the land; the Queen placed a bounty on the dragon's head: a parcel of land and their weight in gold if they could slay the dragon and end its reign of fear.

Rex, a peasant with not a penny to his name, took it upon himself to leave his small village and head to the hills to face the dragon for the grand reward. Knowing the dragon usually hunted at night, Rex approached the dwelling of the beast while the sun was high in the sky. He had made his way through the hills to find a large burrow where the dragon slept. Looking at the dragon's immense size and his feeble weapons, Rex knew he would have to find another way to defeat the creature. Abandoning the cavern, he returned to the road to ponder his options. As the sun set, a woman appeared on the horizon. She was draped in dark robes and he could only see half her face.

“Greetings, weary traveler,” she bowed to him. “I sense a need within you. Perhaps I can be of assistance?”

“How do you know what I need? And what could a random woman give me?” Rex was skeptical as she pulled out 3 vials from her sleeve, each one of vibrant coloring: purple, blue, and gold.

“I bare gifts of power. The blue will give you swift speeds, the purple will grant you immense strength, but the gold…” She slyly grinned. “The gold will grant you the powers of a silver tongue.”

“What cost do you require? I am a peasant, I have nothing to offer,” Rex explained.

“When you have earned your winnings, I will come to find you, you will bestow upon me a small cottage on your lands and the debt will be repaid." The witch, held the vials between her fingers, outstretched to him and shaking them in a taunting manner.

"Deal," he said quickly. He went to take all three vials, but she pulled back, shaking her head.

"Only one," she told him. He took his time before settling on the gold vial. "The gift of gab it is."

Rex took the vial from her, the liquid swirls of gold entranced him; he looked back to thank her but the woman was gone. He waited until nightfall when the beast would awaken to convince the dragon of a compromise confident in the magic the witch had given him.

"Great and magnificent dragon," Rex began after swallowing the potion, waltzing into the burrow. "I ask you to spare my life so that I can spare yours! Men from all over have come to lay siege at your door because the Queen has offered land and money for your death! I offer you instead a bargain...

Allow me to show proof you are slain, and in turn, you can seek refuge on my lands never to be hunted again."

He waited for the ghastly fire breath to kill him, but it did not come. The dragon laughed at him but the nodding of her head filled Rex with delight: the charming effects had worked. She brought up her talon and plucked a giant tooth from her mouth, handing it to Rex.

"Come find me when you have your lands or I will come to find you," the dragon promised, returning to her slumber.

Rex eagerly left the burrow and made his way to the Queen with his bounty. The Queen hung on his every word as he told a false tale of slaying the dragon, the magic of the potion still in effect. Caught up in the pleasures of royalty, Rex forgot about his deals with the witch and dragon, staying with the Queen longer instead of taking up his new lands.

A terrible nightmare woke him a fortnight later: the witch and dragon had both come for him, laying ruin to all that he had been given. He left in the dead of night drenched with fear to uphold his end of the bargains, lest they come and destroy everything. He made his way to the parcel of land he had been given, to work on building the witch her cottage and digging a new lair for the dragon. His construction complete, the witch appeared upon sunset, her smile clear to him.

"A wise man does not let his charm get the better of him," she mused as she passed him to enter her new cottage.

Rex made his way to the hillside to retrieve the dragon after the witch was settled in.

"I was growing impatient," the dragon warned him. "It is good you kept your promise." She offered him her back and took them back to his domain. Upon their return, the weight of fear lifted from Rex, his duties fulfilled and his life no longer in danger from the deals.

CHAPTER TEN
THE WARRIOR

It seemed the stairwell would never end, step by step, clattering of metal to concrete. Torches flickering their flames about in a non-existent wind, lighting the pathway that would lead to the top of the tower. This task would not be easy, devils seemed to lurk beyond every turn and their existence never ceased, and what lay ahead, the gods themselves hardly knew

Within this solid hall of brick with stairs with the air of a warrior about it. Decked in armor of silver and leather, a helmet over the skull for protection, this warrior was not to be taken lightly. A sword rested in his gauntlet covered hands and with every cautious step the air moved nervously, his hold on his weapon only grew more tenacious. This warrior prayed to his gods for help and assistance, as much as they could offer, for it was them that had sent him on his way to this forsaken castle. The terrifying beauty of the place was a trickery, what truly hid within it was devious and evil at its purest.

With brown eyes, feverish with using its sight, glancing every way possible that they could swivel. The eyes were all that could truly be seen as human in this armored one, chocolate eyes of a milky color, even the skin was hidden in the depths of darkness beneath it all. But it was human, the structure showed no sign of an ogre and though tall for one of its age and kind it was no giant. The possibility of it being a demon of any kind was doubtful as the gods would surely never ask for the help of one. There were other races to choose from that this one could be but, alas it was nothing more than a regular human, magic-less but never the less ending its days as a fighter.

The next step took him around a corner and there it finally was, the end of the stairwell, a door of a heavy wooden structure. The door, however, was not the only thing seen, another demonic creature lurked outside the final room, guarding the entrance to the warrior's goal. The devil was aware of his presence and his beady red eyes glinted from the torch beside it. Skin of a wicked black, and hair of an even dark color was clear to see showing just how inhuman he was. It was going to be no easy task defeating this one as the others had been. The demon was even dressed in armor of a kind and magic vibrated off it wildly. Symbols marked his face, trailing down his skin, disappearing beneath his suit, appearing again in places where its natural exterior did show.

"I've been waiting," the devil's voice called out, in the modern dialect. "You have proved yourself worthy to fight me but I can promise you that I will not allow you to walk through this door to my chambers unless your dead body is tossed into it." Dark scaled leather wings appeared from his back as he stepped closer to the warrior. Horns protruded from his temple as a short yell erupted from his vocal cords out of his mouth, a tail sprouting from his back.

The warrior returned no words in exchange to the threat but his eyes narrowed and he tightened his grip upon the hilt of his sword and placed his body into a battle stance. His right leg was forward as his left leg hung back, and his sword was held firmly in front of him.

The demon wasted no time in charging at him, beginning the fight that would lead the warrior to his final task. The demon used his body as a weapon, arms, legs, and tail morphing into weapons or using their sharp edges as knives. The battle seemed to last for hours, and the warrior was exhausted but giving up would mean certain death while continuing would give some hope of survival. The two shared their fair share of wounds, the demon suffered more open wounds and the human suffered from bruises and dull pains. The devil had yet to unleash his magic, the kind he was well capable of.

The warriors back faced the door and the demon's faced the emptiness that the stairwell held. They were several feet apart, both breathing heavily, it seemed like a break, it didn't last long. A black hand outstretched itself in front of the devil and a black orb outlined in a white blinding color formed within his palm. The eyes of the human widened in horror, knowing what was to come, but there was nothing to block with, hide behind, or run to, he had to take the hit.

And so, he did.

The powerful blast of magic threw him into the door, it cracked from the force. The crack gave way, though, and the entrance to the room was open. The warrior was then thrown into the wall across from the door, covered in what should have been metal but instead the leather attire beneath it, that had little padding for the human body under it. The metal armor was all gone, the sword that he once held as well, destroyed into nothing from the magic blast of the demon. His body slumped to the ground, head low, neck bending as far as possible, till the human's chin touched his chest, and long silver hair fell out from behind his ears in front of the face.

The demon cursed, he hadn't meant to break the door but he continued in, all the same. The room was nothing but a chamber, a bed, a vanity, furniture of an average sort but decorated with intricate designs, except for a golden chest to the side that made the room appear different. When his maniacal red eyes landed on his prey he gasped and made a furious cry.

His opponent was no man as he had thought him to be but a woman! But it did not matter now, as it appeared our warrior, man or woman was dead, or so the demon had assumed.

A groan echoed from her lips and a quivering hand steadied itself on the cold ground. The head rose as did her whole form. The bruises and cuts were more evident without the silver armor. Her brown eyes met his glowing red ones almost in a challenging manner as her lips stretched into a smirk.

"YOU!" the devil shouted, pointing angrily. "How could you be alive? Are you some sort of immortal? No mere human can withstand my power!"

"But alas, evil one, I am but pure flesh and bone of a mortal, and it is I who shall be your demise," The woman said bringing her hand to her face wiping at her mouth, checking for blood. A chuckle sounded from her as another infuriated holler echoed within the room. "Do calm yourself, foul spawn of Hell...You are not the first nor the last of your kind to be dispatched by a mortal, a female mortal at that!"

"I'll kill you, you wench!" The devil charged as he had once before, but his madness would be his fall, as it was blinding.

She moved out of his pathway and he collided into the wall but jumped off from it, leaping at her again, she dodged this as well. The cat and mouse game carried on for a while and no victor came to be as neither landed an attack over the next hour. The woman could dodge no more and this was clear when his clawed hand made contact with her side.

She cried out in pain as her attempted dodge lead her to land on the ground itself. Her breathing was heavy as she staggered up to escape another taloned hand that dug into the stone where she had fallen.

"Hah! You are but a mortal, you tire so easily," he pointed out triumphantly as he had forced her to a corner. Her eyes darted around the room; she had no weapon. The room was a mess, the furniture was destroyed and tossed about aimlessly. She saw a window but jumping wasn't the option, nor could she fit his large form through it. "You know," he hissed, he was barely a foot away, "You aren't that bad looking, and I haven't had a woman's flesh in a while." He licked his dark lips tentatively. She felt her eyes getting heavy from the loss of blood and if she didn't do something quickly, she'd pass out and for sure it would all be over.

She released her blood dripping side and rammed her shoulder into his chest, something he hadn't expected, it was quite a rash decision. It brought him to the ground with her on top of him. She blocked his clawing hands with her arm, his talons cutting her deep. Her other hand reached for his tail, it was sharp-pointed and stubborn, but she caught it and pulled hard.

The tail came off of his body with a hard jolt, tiring her immensely and her sight blacked suddenly in flashes. While she was drifting in and out of consciousness he changed the stakes and rolled her over so that he was on top of her. A new tail sprouted from his spine, as though what she had done had been of no effect, but she hadn't done it to hurt him, no. She had done it to use against him. The woman finally got a hold of herself and held the tail tightly like a dagger and drove it into the demon's chest repeatedly.

He became still from the impalement. Blue thick blood coated her front as she pushed his limp body off of her. She was immobile herself, eyes attempting to blink away the darkness that her eyes threatened to release. The floor around her was a clash of a rainbow, her maroon blood, the demons deep blue goop, and the mixture of the two forming a purple like color.

She awoke in the comfort of her bed, bandages wrapping most of her body. She ached and dared not move. There was mirth in her though, laughing at the luck that she may live from a quest she certainly thought she would die for. She had fought with what she believed was her last breath and now she was breathing air while that devil rotted.

CONCLUSION

You've bested foes, dealt deals with dragons, swam in the deepest trenches of the ocean, and I hope you've dreamed of more spectacular fantasies. These adult bedtime stories have been here for your peace of mind to be your grownup lullabies. Pick these up anytime you have trouble sleeping again to whisk you away to a deep slumber.

If you enjoyed this book, please let me know your thoughts by leaving a short review on Audible.. Thank you!